Making Room
Leader Guide

Making Room
Sharing the Love of Christmas
Leader Guide

Making Room
978-1-7910-0637-2
978-1-7910-0638-9 eBook

Making Room Leader Guide
978-1-7910-0639-6
978-1-7910-0640-2 eBook

ED ROBB

MAKING ROOM

SHARING THE LOVE OF CHRISTMAS

LEADER GUIDE

BY VICTORIA REBECK

Abingdon Press | Nashville

MAKING ROOM: LEADER GUIDE

ISBN-13: 978-1-7910-0639-6

20 21 22 23 24 25 26 27 28 29—10 9 8 7 6 5 4 3 2 1
MANUFACTURED IN THE UNITED STATES OF AMERICA

CONTENTS

INTRODUCTION

Advent is a season of hope or a season of darkness; perhaps it is both simultaneously. The church has for generations observed Advent as a time to prepare our hearts and lives to receive the gift of a vulnerable infant, Immanuel, who is the personification of God's love. For some, it is a time of excitement and joy as they prepare to see friends and family. Many enjoy decorating their homes, choosing the right Christmas gifts for others, or volunteering to help serve meals for those who could use a warm dinner served by kind people.

For others, Advent is a time of disappointment, bad memories, or loneliness. The darkening days of December in the northern hemisphere further cast their mood into shadows.

It is also sometimes the forgotten season. Church activities and retail establishments beckon us to go directly to Christmas Day, taking away the opportunity to contemplate and consider what the coming of Christ really means to our own lives and to the world.

This Leader Guide is designed to be used with the Advent study *Making Room: Sharing the Love of Christmas* by Ed Robb.

Reverend Robb is senior pastor of The Woodlands United Methodist Church in Houston, Texas. Serving the church for more than forty years, his vision and leadership have led the church to become one of the fastest growing churches in Methodism, with more than fourteen thousand members. He has helped Christians deepen their celebrations of Christmas through his books *The Wonder of Christmas: Once You Believe, Anything Is Possible* (Abingdon Press, 2016) and *Under Wraps: The Gift We Never Expected* (Abingdon Press, 2014). He has also inspired Christians through his book *Mountaintop Moments: Meeting God in the High Places* (Abingdon Press, 2019), which connects personal mountaintop experiences in our spiritual life with the mountains in the Old and New Testaments and the events related to those sacred places. He and his wife, Beverley, have three adult children.

Robb's thoughtful observations about how God moves through the ancient story of Christmas and our present experiences help us reclaim this soulful season. *Making Room* points us to the light, hospitality, and love of God in the Scripture stories that prepare us for Jesus's birth. Recalling beloved memories of childhood Sundays spent at his grandparents' small, rural Methodist congregation—characterized by sumptuous meals in the church fellowship hall, loving members who helped one another with the complications that arise in everyone's lives, and members who cared about and knew all the children in the congregation—Robb sheds light on the Christmas story themes of loving our neighbors, welcoming strangers, inviting people into our circles of relationships, and guiding others into the loving community of God and God's people. Some research has suggested that Americans are isolated, lonely, and hungry for friends, while neighbors barely know each other. Did Mary and

They were not welcomed.

Joseph, who traveled a long way to Bethlehem for the census, feel the same way when they entered a crowded town where there were no guest rooms available?

After Jesus's birth, the Holy Family found that they had to welcome strangers, even at that difficult time. Lowly shepherds and stately magi visited the family in their meager shelter. Robb sees in this a model of welcoming strangers and, in so doing, meeting others who would be their friends and supporters. *as opposed to the*

Part of welcoming others is to "leave a light on," showing them where they might find shelter, warmth, and a meal. In a world where the darkness of violence, oppression, and greed threatens to overwhelm lives, offering the love of God sheds a light that vanquishes the darkness. The star that pointed others to the place of Jesus's birth was just such a sign of hospitality. It proclaimed that the realm of God makes room for every person on earth. *home that turned its lights off and hid behind the couch on Halloween. :)*

Almost everyone has an experience of getting lost, whether it is not knowing one's way out of unfamiliar territory or losing sight of what brings meaning and purpose to one's life. That is why God made humans to be social beings. We need God, and we need each other. When one of us is hurting, others can provide comfort. When one of us rejoices, others can join us in celebration. And when we see the systematic dehumanizing of others, such as when nations or leaders allow hunger, abuse, neglect, and other forms of violence and hate to destroy lives, we are, together, able to do more to overcome this than we would alone, each by ourselves. We are guides for one another, leading back to God's love and a community that puts first those who have been beaten down or forgotten.

The four themes in *Making Room* overlap, and Robb weaves them together with stories, personal experiences, and reflections on Scripture. For those who seek a renewing moment of sabbath and reflection before Christmas, a group study of *Making Room* will provide that, along with the companionship of others who wish to grow closer to God and offer compassion to others.

How to Use This Guide

This guide is a map to help you lead a group to explore these themes and to bring to them the group's own experiences and stories. Sharing their observations, questions, and prayers, the group members will support and encourage one another to grow closer to God and to care about their neighbors in tangible ways so that the world is transformed into the realm of God.

You may follow the format precisely and thus offer informative background as well as raise questions for fruitful reflection and discussion. But, this guide is flexible and can be adapted to your own purposes. You may adapt it to your preferred method of group facilitation as well as add information that you have found through research you did to prepare for this study. Choose among the questions and activities that you find most appropriate to your group. You may find that each group, even if from the same church, will benefit from a different set of activities or questions.

Planning the Meeting

Group size: This study works best when it is used in small gatherings. A group of six to twelve people may be optimal, as it allows time for all to share their thoughts. If a number of people are interested in participating—which is a positive development—start more than one group and train more than one person to lead the groups.

Invite mark/ERIN to come to study +

Length of sessions: The main book and this companion study guide have four sections. This matches the number of weeks in the Advent season. Therefore, a meeting once per week is optimal. Because this is only a four-week study, many participants will find that they can make this short-term commitment.

The leader should uphold the agreed-upon time frame for the meetings. We suggest sixty to ninety minutes. This would allow for ample discussion time while respecting participants' personal plans and obligations. This is especially important for those who are already very busy during this season. The study should help people engage in Advent, not make it more burdensome.

Day of week: Identify a day and time of week that most participants will be able to accommodate. Do not limit considerations to evenings. Many people prefer not to drive at night, after a long day at work, or when they have to help children with homework or engage in other daily household chores. If most find one evening a week to be most convenient, then identify which evening will be best. Others will prefer afternoons, weekends, or a mealtime. Ask those interested in participating what their preferred meeting times would be. A word of caution, however: do not get overly involved in trying to accommodate every participant. Do your best to pick a day and time that works for the participants, but let them know that you may not be able to please everyone.

Participants: Most who express interest will be people who are already regular attenders of your church's worship services. However, encourage them to invite friends and family members. There are many people who wish for more interaction and hope during what, for some, is a dark time of year. Others may be curious to know of a religious community that is truly loving and welcoming, asks honest questions, and respects everyone's experiences. Even a brief experience like this can make a great difference to someone.

Materials: Two to four weeks before the first meeting, help participants obtain the book. Ask them to read the book's introduction and chapter 1 in advance. The introduction is important, for it sets the foundation for the book. It is an engaging read, as it includes stories that readers may identify with.

Read before 1st Wed, Dec 1st

Location: You might choose a central location where participants are used to gathering, such as the church building. Another option is in participants' homes. For reasons of public health, weather, or distances, you might consider using an online meeting platform. (All participants should have internet access and be comfortable using the meeting platform.) Regardless of the location, it should be quiet, free from interruption from family members and pets, and private.

Tips for Online Meetings

Meeting online is a great option for a number of situations. During a time of illness or inclement weather, online meetings are a welcome opportunity for folks to converse while seeing each other's faces. Online meetings can also give those who do not have access to transportation or who prefer not to travel at certain times of day the chance to participate. Finally, these meetings expand the "neighborhood" of possible group members since people can log in from just about anywhere in the world.

There are a number of platforms for online meetings. Search the internet for "web conferencing software," and you will find plenty from which to choose.

Training and Practice

- Choose a platform and practice using it so that you are comfortable with it. Engage in a couple of practice runs with another person.
- Set up a training meeting to teach participants how to log in (if necessary) and to use the tools available with the program.
- For those who do not have internet service, let them know they may telephone into the meeting and provide them the number.

The Real Meetings

- **Early invitations.** Send out invitations at least a week in advance. Many meeting platforms enable you to do this through their software.
- **Early log in.** Participants should log in at least ten minutes in advance, to test their audio and their video connections.
- **Muting.** Instruct participants to keep their microphones muted during the meeting so that extraneous noise from their location does not interrupt the meeting. This includes chewing or yawning sounds, which can be embarrassing!
- **Signaling.** When it is time for discussion, participants can unmute themselves. However, ask them to raise their hand or wave when they are ready to share so that you can call on them. Give folks a few minutes to speak up. They may not be used to conversing in web conferences.

- **Show and tell.** Make good use of visual media since listening only to audio can get boring. Show artwork, crèche scenes, cartoons, children's drawings, and so on. Make sure your lit candle and other "worship table" decor are visible. When you feel adept at doing so, you can show appropriate videos you find on the internet. Consider posting Advent-related art or wall hangings in the background of the room where you are participating.

Options to Consider

Prayer journals. The practice of keeping a journal while reading the week's chapter can enhance reflection and more extensive interaction outside the group sessions. You can promote the use of a journal by using one of your own as part of your preparation and class time. Group members can use any sort of book they would like for journaling: composition books, bound book with blank pages, sheets of loose-leaf paper, or electronic documents they prepare on their computers or tablets. Others may prefer to make notes in the margins of the book.

Some groups even use dedicated internet sites where they can post ideas and share thoughts. Google Docs is one such site. This approach gives you a permanent record of what you have learned and where you still have questions.

Encourage those who decide to use the journal to reflect on the reading, write questions for future learning, and consider commitments they might make for their own spiritual growth. They may even want to keep the journal with them throughout their day, in case they have insights or inspirations related to the topic that they want to capture.

Invite those who keep such a journal to bring their journals to group meetings. This can remind them of thoughts and questions they had during the week. They may also choose to add information and insights they've gained during sessions.

Artistic expression. Some people communicate their spiritual thoughts through art. Encourage group members, if they wish, to draw, paint, sculpt, or otherwise create something that speaks to the themes of the book. Others may want to write poetry or compose a song. Ask them to share these with the group, if they are comfortable doing so.

events or post cards

Connections with church activities. Your church will likely have other Advent activities and observations. Instead of competing with these, consider how you might integrate them into the study and its themes. Ask your church leaders for a calendar of these church activities to share with your group.

Your group members may not plan to attend all or any of these. You may want to encourage those who attend at least a few of them to look for connections between the focuses of the activities and the emphases of the study. Ask them about the commonalities or contrasts they observed. For instance, if your church decorates a Chrismon tree, look at the symbols used. Do any of them relate to concepts that the author of *Making Room* raises? In what ways?

Another example: The children of the church may perform a pageant during Advent. Did the study group members notice if the play demonstrated the themes of being a neighbor, welcoming strangers, inviting others into a community of caring people, or guiding one another on our spiritual pathways?

Conducting the Sessions

The Meeting Environment

- Meetings should take place in a quiet, comfortable space away from interruptions.
- Participants should silence their phones.
- Arrange seating in a circle or other configuration that allows participants to see one another's faces.
- If you are meeting through an online conferencing platform, ask participants to make advance preparations to prevent interruptions from telephones, family members, pets, noise, and so on. If possible, they should join the meeting in a closed room. Remind them to mute their microphone when they are not speaking. Ask them to log in at least ten minutes before the meeting starts to test their audio and video.

Materials You Will Need

- A candle (can be battery operated) for use during the opening prayer time.
- Other relevant visual elements for the altar table, as desired. Items that communicate welcome, companionship, guidance, and acceptance would be particularly appropriate. A crèche is very fitting. Perhaps group members would like to take turns bringing their own for the altar table each week.
- Pens for taking notes.
- Optional flip chart for highlighting discussion comments.

- Extra Bibles for those who may not have brought one to the meeting.
- If meeting online, ask participants to bring to their tables a candle of their own as well as some objects (crosses, art) that communicate the presence of God to them. Remind them to bring their copy of *Making Room*, a pen and pad for notes, their journal (if they are keeping one), and a Bible.

Discussion Leadership Guidelines

- Keep in mind that some people will jump right in with answers and comments, while others need time to process what is being discussed. Encourage the eager talkers to wait a moment or two to allow others to speak. If you notice that some group members seem never to be able to enter the conversation, ask them if they have thoughts to share. Give everyone a chance to talk, but keep the conversation moving. Moderate to prevent a few individuals from doing all the talking.
- Communicate the importance of group discussions and group exercises.
- If a discussion question does not elicit immediate response, allow time for silence. Participants may need some time to ponder. Count silently to ten, then say something such as, "Would anyone like to go first?" If no one responds, venture a response yourself and ask for comments. Remember, you are not looking

for "the right answer." Participants' honest expressions of their hearts and minds will be the source of the most learning and growing for the whole group.

- Model openness as you share with the group. Establish a foundation of honesty and trust. Group members will follow your example. If you limit your sharing to a surface level, others will do likewise.

- Share some questions you may have that the readings prompted. Ask the group if they've had similar questions and what they think. This reinforces the character of the study as an opportunity for mutual learning, which happens during sessions and beyond.

- Encourage multiple answers or responses before moving on to the next topic or question. Avoid asking, "What does this story mean?," which participants may conclude to mean that there is one correct answer. Instead, ask, "What does this story mean to you?" Just as the Gospels show that there is more than one way to tell the story of Jesus's birth, there is more than one perspective on its significance. It is the mosaic of many perceptions that constitute the greater picture.

- To help continue a discussion and give it greater depth, follow up to some responses with statements like "Tell us what led you to this observation" or "Tell us more about that."

- Affirm participants' contributions to the discussion, especially when they have offered something personal or have spoken up in group for the first time. You might respond with comments such as "Good insight," "I never thought of that before," "I'm glad you mentioned that," or whatever makes sense to you in that moment.

- Monitor your own contributions. If you are doing most of the talking, back off so that you do not train the group to listen rather than to speak up. And remember, this is not an opportunity to turn the conversations back to what you want to say. As much as possible, establish an environment in which the participants contribute the majority of the discussion content.
- Remember that you do not have all the answers. Your job is to keep the discussion going and encourage participation.

Before Each Meeting

- **Pray.** You are on an important journey. Pray for God's guidance as you discern and lead. Also pray for the members of your group.
- **Familiarize yourself with the content.** Read the book chapter, the Bible verses, and the week's session plan. Take note of any special preparations, such as providing musical accompaniment, bringing special objects, and so on. Take your time with the Scripture reading, paying attention to aspects of the text you have not noticed before. Consider reading more than one translation since, as Robb

points out, translations differ in the words they use, where they end sentences, and more.

- **Determine which of the suggested activities and discussion questions you will use.** Think about which are most appropriate for your group, and make those a priority. Be sure to ask your group what activities they are finding most helpful. Of course, use activities and questions that you have devised for the group. Be prepared, however, to adjust the session as group members interact and questions arise. Often members will raise concerns or interests that prove to be important to the group.

- **Think ahead about how you might respond to the questions.** Do not think you have to have an "answer" to them. They are designed to prompt reflection and imagination. Given members' personal experiences and background, they may well interpret and adapt the study content differently. Those differences provide additional opportunities for listening and supporting one another and for deepening our own understanding of God and our place in building God's realm on earth.

Expectations for Participants

- **Read assignments.** Participants are to read one chapter per group session from *Making Room*. A significant part of adult learning is sharing what you know. Thus, adults are as much the teachers as the learners. Participants gain the most insight from one another's perceptions and sharing their own experiences.

- **Interact respectfully.** The study group should be a safe place where participants agree to speak honestly and respectfully, to listen without interrupting, and to honor the time so that each participant who wishes to speak has the opportunity to do so. The leader plays the primary role in promoting this practice.

- **Bring *Making Room* and a Bible.** Reinforce to the group the importance of bringing these books to each meeting. The leader should provide some extra Bibles at group meetings for those who may not have brought one. If some participants do not own a Bible, encourage them to visit www.cokesbury.com, where they can find affordable choices. Suggest a couple of interpretations for them, as they may be overwhelmed by the many options.

- **Bring pens, pencils, and paper for notes.** A significant source of learning and growing from this study takes place in group discussion. Taking notes in notebooks or in the margins of the book can help participants consider questions and insights that come out of the meeting.

Session Guide Outline

Each session contains the following elements:

- **Session Goals.** These provide purpose for the discussions.

- **Reading Assignments.** Participants should read the next session's chapter from *Making Room* in advance.
- **Centering Prayer.** This short liturgy can begin the sessions. It helps participants calm their minds and spirits and center their attention.
- **Scripture and Biblical Insights.** Relevant Bible passages are suggested to help participants draw their own theological connections with Robb's reflections.
- **Review of the Session's Readings.** These are highlights of the session's chapter to read aloud (or invite others to read) as a reminder for participants.
- **Questions for Discussion.** Prioritize the questions that the group will find most engaging.
- **Closing Prayer.** This sends the participants into the world to practice what they have learned in the study.

Session Topics

Session 1—Be a Neighbor

God's love is mediated to us and our neighbors through relationships—most significantly through our relationship with Jesus. Participants will look closely at their own relationships—be they close, casual, or estranged—and determine how they can share God's love through them.

Session 2—Welcome Strangers

God calls us into relationship not only with friends and family but especially with people who are new to the arenas of our lives, whether they are just passing through or have come to stay. Mary and Joseph relied upon hospitality from others and offered it themselves. Participants will compare their practices of hospitality with the biblical models and consider how to expand their ministry of inviting and welcoming the stranger.

Session 3—Leave the Light On

Advent comes to the northern hemisphere in a time of diminishing daylight. The long dark nights sometimes intensify a sense of discouragement, disappointment, or grief. The star of Bethlehem reminds us that God breaks into our darkness with light that welcomes us and guides us. Invite participants to consider where they can "leave the light on" for those who feel lonely or despondent.

Session 4—Walk Each Other Home

Life can take some unexpected turns that leave us feeling lost and uncertain about how we will move forward. Jesus came not only to bring us new life but also to walk alongside us in life, leading us through valleys of shadows to places of comfort and peace. Stories of Jesus's companionship and guidance will inspire participants to find ways in which they can be a companion and listener for others who are searching for a way "home"—to a place of hope and belonging in the community of God's people.

At Advent, people sometimes find that they have little energy or attention to wait expectantly for the coming of Christ. Family and social events, preparations, and planning church events can distract them from the spiritual joys of the time. Pondering themes of light, hospitality, and a guiding star can help churchgoers and seekers discover deeper significance in the stories of Jesus's birth and a meaningful alternative to the superficiality and consumerism that sometimes overshadow Christmas. This study will encourage them to be the light and companionship of God for others.

Session 1

BE A NEIGHBOR

Beginning the Series

This is the first time the group will meet together. Welcome participants. Introduce yourself and ask them to introduce themselves. Tell them a story about how you have observed Advent in the past. Even if the answer is "I haven't," provide that honest answer. That will help them know that it is OK not to feel "Christmas-y." Ask if others have their own traditions, such as lighting Advent candles weekly, putting out crèches, or observing St. Nicholas's Day. Ask them what interested them in joining this group study.

Let them know the length of each session (ninety minutes may be optimal) and that sessions will move in this order:

- Centering Prayer
- Scripture
- Biblical Insights
- Review of the Session's Readings
- Questions for Discussion
- Closing Prayer

Group Covenant

Remind the participants that when groups engage in discussions of faith, the gathering should be a safe place for honest and gracious sharing.

Provide copies of the covenant (below) to each participant. Invite them to read it aloud, each person taking turns reading one of the "we will" promises.

Ask the participants if they would agree to this covenant. Would they add anything? Ask them to read the list aloud together.

- We agree to speak honestly and respectfully.
- We will share from our own experiences as we feel comfortable doing so.
- We will not speak for others or correct or judge what they say.
- We will listen without interrupting.
- We will not attempt to solve others' expressed problems.
- We will honor the time so that each participant who wishes to speak has the opportunity to do so. We will honor the leader's request to finish our comments so another can share.
- We will make sure that others have opportunities to speak. Also, we will respect others' decisions not to speak.
- We will pray for each other between meetings.

Invite them to suggest other practices they would find helpful.

Introduction to the Significance of Advent

Research the history of Advent and share anything of interest with your participants. Explain that Advent helps us recommit to God and God's people so that we are ready to receive the newborn Jesus, who came as a child and the savior of the world. This is not unlike when John the Baptist called people to repent, to turn back to God, to prepare for the beginning of Christ's saving and renewing ministry.

Theme Verse

So they hurried off and found Mary and Joseph, and the baby, who was lying in the manger. When they had seen him, they spread the word concerning what had been told them about this child, and all who heard it were amazed at what the shepherds said to them. But Mary treasured up all these things and pondered them in her heart. The shepherds returned, glorifying and praising God for all the things they had heard and seen, which were just as they had been told.

Luke 2:16-20

Session Goals

The conversations and activities in this session will equip participants to

- adopt an intentional practice of Advent observance.
- grasp the recognition that we know God's love through relationships.
- learn to look for and recognize the overlooked and lonely in the world.

Reading Assignments

Before this session, participants should read

- the introduction and chapter 1 of *Making Room*
- Luke 2:1-20

Encourage them to read these when they have time to read them carefully and pray over them. Remind them a few days in advance of the session to read the passages, if they have not yet had time to do so.

Centering Prayer

Light the candle and invite participants to center their spirits and hearts for this time of worship as you pray.

> *God of light, God in my neighbor: Still our hearts, calm our spirits. Help us listen as you speak. As Jesus invited us into life with you and your people, show us how to invite and welcome others. In the name of Christ, we pray. Amen.*

Scripture

Read aloud the following Scripture passages: Luke 2:1-20; Luke 14:7-14; Psalm 133.

Give participants a minute or two to ponder these passages. Then pray:

> *Your word is a lamp that lights our way, our God. No matter how far we run, your light will shine upon us and lead us back to you. May you give us eyes to see truth in your light. Amen.*

[handwritten margin note: This is only possible in the pouring out of the Holy Spirit, just like the oil mentioned]

Biblical Insights

Reread aloud (or invite one or two participants to do so) Luke 2:1-20.

Invite participants to discuss these or other questions. Be sure to keep track of time so that the group has the opportunity to discuss the reading as well. Ask fewer questions if the group is particularly inclined to share their thoughts and experiences.

- What struck you as you heard this story again?
- What does that seem to be saying to you?

Verses 16 through 20 tell us about the shepherds' response to Jesus's birth as well as Mary's response to the shepherds.

- What do you imagine Mary was thinking?
- What do you imagine you would be thinking or feeling if you were Joseph or Mary in this situation?
- The angels could have told anyone about the birth of Jesus. In Luke's telling, the announcement goes first to the shepherds. Why do you suppose this is? Who else might the angels have told?
- Who, if anyone, is a neighbor in this story? What would you say makes them a neighbor?
- Think back to when you were growing up. Do you remember a hierarchy among your classmates—who was "in" and who was "out"? Do you see this in groups at this point in your life?
- Do you see a correlation between the story that Jesus tells in Luke 14 and his relationships, which are sometimes adversarial, with Pharisees?
- Can you think of ways you can counter favoritism and privilege in your community or home? Or even church?

- Our psalm today talks about the blessing of God's people living in unity. How would you define *unity*? What are the conditions and practices that make unity possible?
- Sometimes there are differences of opinion among God's people that result in hurt feelings and hurtful words or actions. In what ways do you think you can be part of building reconciliation and respect?

Review of the Session's Readings

Ed Robb remembers his grandparents' church, which he visited as a child. It seemed like everyone knew and cared about one another. Fellowship time after worship was like a family feast: people talking, people laughing, people offering a listening ear to those who were hurting. "Looking back, the fellowship hall seemed to me to be twice as large as the church's sanctuary," he says in the book's introduction. "But that's not surprising really since it held the heart and spirit of Christian community within its walls."

He reminds us that Christian faith is most often practiced in the context of community. Holy Communion, which we take as a community of faith in the presence of God, teaches us that. John Wesley, who founded Methodism with his brother Charles, talked about "social holiness," meaning that he believed that God made humans to be social beings. Through the two Great Commandments—love God and love your neighbor—Jesus told us that it is in relationships that we live out our faith. This is especially true in our relationships with other Christians but also very true for our relationships with others, as the Bible frequently reminds us.

Yet it can be difficult to be a good neighbor. Understanding that in the literal sense—the people who are near us in proximity—Robb tells a story about how he and his wife, Bev, realized that, even though they had lived in their house for many years, they knew few of their neighbors. They made some extra effort to invite them into their home at Advent, and in so doing, created some neighborhood connectedness.

Somehow, meals seem to often be at the center of gatherings. The small-church potluck lunches, the neighborhood barbecues, celebrations—food is present when people get together. Robb points out that when the Book of Acts speaks of the early church, it mentions that they shared meals together in their homes and shared everything in common. When Jesus and a small boy fed five thousand on five loaves and two fish, there was still some left over. It's a simple feast, but everyone gets to eat. And the last book of the Bible, the Book of Revelation, ends with a depiction of a glorious wedding feast.

Just because someone is our "neighbor" in some way does not mean we find them likable. Robb points to a remark from C. S. Lewis, a beloved author and apologist, who says that we need not decide if we *feel* like we love our neighbor. We are called to *act* like we love our neighbor. Often, as we have practiced that for a while, we develop an actual love for our neighbor.

Questions for Discussion

- When have you reached out in neighborly concern for someone?
- There are neighbors who live near us, and there are people who are our neighbors in other ways. Whom do you think of as "neighbors," and why?

When has someone been a neighbor to you?

- Is there someone in your life who has been a good neighbor to you in some way—whether or not this person lived near you?
- Tell about a time when you felt discouraged. Did anyone reach out to you? How did you feel about that?
- Robb points out the many times that meals are mentioned in the Bible when a gathering of people is described. Can you think of more examples?
- Can you think of times when meals were an important part of gatherings, large or small, that you have attended? What difference did sharing a meal make in the situation? Do you find that meals make a difference to your spiritual life?
- Think about a favorite Advent hymn—one that looks ahead to Jesus's birth, not one that celebrates that his birth has happened. Why do you think it is your favorite? Take a moment to ponder this question before you answer it: Does this song happen to describe something that would apply to our being a good neighbor?

Closing Prayer

End the session with a bidding prayer. Explain that at certain times in the prayer you will invite people to speak aloud (or silently in their hearts) a name or place for which they would offer prayer. Because of time constraints, this is not a time for each person to offer their own complete prayer.

Remind the group not to raise names of people known to others in the congregation who have not given permission or have not shared their prayer request publicly. Further, all prayer requests, like all discussion in these sessions, should be confidential.

A sample bidding prayer:

> *Our loving God, you reach out to us and call us to your side. We are blessed to have neighbors in our lives, be those people we know and love, people we don't care for, people we hear about on news reports, or people we do not know yet. Because we experience your love, as neighbors we humbly pray for ourselves, our friends and family, and people in nations around the world.*
>
> *We pray for these family members:*
>
> *We pray for these friends:*
>
> *We pray for those who suffer or are in trouble:*
>
> *We praise you for these reasons for giving thanks:*
>
> *We pray for these concerns of our communities:*
>
> *We pray for the church's mission and its leaders:*
>
> *We pray for needs around the world:*
>
> *With confidence in your love, we offer these prayers to you and each other, the body of Christ. Show us how we can be representatives of your love and forgiveness. Amen.*

Prepare them for the next session:

- Thank the group for their contributions to the discussion.
- Remind them to read chapter 2 for the next session.
- Ask them to bring an object, song, poem, or story that they associate with anticipating the birth of Christ. [Leader: plan to do this as well.]

Homework: Bring an ornament that's significant to you.

You can spend a moment to tell us why.

Offer a sending forth, such as: "Go forth to love God and to be the neighbor that Jesus was to those he encountered."

Encourage participants to exchange signs and words of peace with one another as they leave.

Be sure to extinguish the candle. If meeting online, remind participants to extinguish their candles.

Session 2

WELCOME STRANGERS

Opening the Session

- Welcome participants.
- Remind participants briefly about the meeting room environment (see the introduction to this study), especially if the meeting is a virtual (online) one.
- Remind them briefly about their covenant.

Theme Verse

"But you, Bethlehem Ephrathah,
  though you are small among the clans of Judah,
out of you will come for me
    one who will be ruler over Israel."

Micah 5:2

Session Goals

The conversations and activities in this session will equip participants to

- challenge themselves about what the Bible teaches us about being a neighbor.
- look intentionally for the strangers they encounter and reach out to them with caring words and actions.

Reading Assignments

Before this session, participants should read

- chapter 2 of *Making Room*
- Matthew 2:13-23

Encourage them to read these when they have time to read them carefully and pray over them. Remind them a few days in advance of the session to read the passages, if they have not yet had time to do so. Also remind them to bring an object, song, poem, or story that they associate with anticipating the birth of Christ.

Centering Prayer

Light the candle and invite participants to center their spirits and hearts for this time of worship as you pray.

> *God of the stranger, we recall how Mary and Joseph traveled far from their home to a temporary stay in Bethlehem and how difficult that was. Keep us ever mindful of those who come into our lives, for either a brief time or to stay, that we may extend the heart of Christ to them. Amen.*

Scripture

Read aloud the following Scripture passages: Matthew 2:13-23; Jeremiah 29:4-7; Psalm 61:1-5.

Give participants a minute or two to ponder these passages. Then pray:

> *You know our thoughts and our hearts, Creator. You extend mercy and new life when we turn to you. Let our words and thoughts be pleasing to you, Lord, because when we live in you, we are not strangers, but friends. Amen.*

Biblical Insights

Reread aloud (or invite one or two participants to do so) Matthew 2:13-23; Jeremiah 29:4-7; Psalm 61:1-5.

Invite participants to discuss these or other questions. Be sure to keep track of time so that the group has the opportunity to discuss the reading as well. Ask fewer questions if the group is particularly inclined to share their thoughts and experiences.

The Jeremiah passage speaks to a time when the people of Israel were in exile. They had been removed from their homes by an invading army and taken forcibly to Babylon. Though they must have been longing for home, God directed them to settle in, build their homes, raise their children, and contribute to the health and strength of the city.

Tell about a time you were new somewhere. Perhaps you had to move often as part of a military or clergy family. Perhaps you left your home town for a job or school. Or perhaps you were suffering abuse or other hostility that drove you away to a safer place.

- What did it feel like to be new?
- What was life like those first few weeks?
- Did anyone reach out to you?
- What did you learn from this experience?

The verses from Matthew address the Holy Family being strangers in a strange land.

- Can you imagine what Mary and Joseph might have felt when they had to flee danger and go to a strange place? How do you think that felt to them?
- Do you know of other situations in the world where people have had to flee their homes because of danger?
- Have you ever felt like the psalmist did, needing to seek refuge in God? What was that like?
- In what ways may you have provided a refuge for someone going through a difficult time in their lives?

The Micah passage says that from the small, insignificant town of Bethlehem will come a king over Israel. God could have chosen as king someone who would have the solid preparation provided by a good education and opportunities to interact with other powerful leaders. Why would God choose as king someone who was born and raised in meager conditions?

Review of the Session's Readings

Author Ed Robb looks at the many crèche scenes his wife collects and thinks about how many characters are crowded into a small stall with Mary, Joseph, and Jesus. Though there is no evidence that the magi and the shepherds all came at the same time—soon after the baby was born—we often envision it happening that way. Robb asks us to imagine what that would have been like: a brand-new mother and father having to entertain guests. Whenever the shepherds and the magi, and perhaps other visitors, did arrive, it seems they were welcomed by the family.

Hospitality is not only about how the guests feel about being welcomed. The act of welcoming people benefits the hosts as well. Robb suggests that the hosts may gain the most from the experience, that offering hospitality provides its own reward.

We may look forward to inviting guests into our home. But what about strangers—people we barely know? Are we prepared to welcome them into our lives, our circle of friends, or our church?

He tells a story he read about a young woman who was in the grocery store when she learned that her beloved grandfather had died. She was so shocked that she could barely speak or move. Other shoppers (strangers to her) noticed that she was in distress. They called a friend for her and waited with her until she arrived. They bought her groceries and sent them along with her. A few days later, they sent her a flower arrangement through her friend. Though she still mourns her grandfather, she is also comforted by the unexpected care she received from strangers. Their kind acts made a lifelong difference to her.

Welcoming does not always need to be that elaborate. Robb heard from a parishioner a story about how she met her neighbor, an older lady named Gladys. When this young mother would hear Gladys opening the door to leave for her morning walk, she would open the window and wish Gladys a good morning.

Over time this led the women to develop a significant bond of friendship. Eventually Gladys moved away, but the two women stayed in touch. And Gladys will from time to time remind her friend that her simple morning greeting made her feel as though someone cared about her.

The Gospel of Matthew tells how Herod, feeling threatened by the news that a king had just been born, tried to trick the magi into telling him where he could find the infant king. The magi were warned in a dream not to return through Herod's city. An angel warned Mary and Joseph too, and they fled to Egypt for safety—a place where people did not practice Judaism nor speak the language Mary and Joseph spoke. They were strangers in a strange land.

Such stories can inspire us to look for the strangers in our midst. We can seek those who feel lonely and neglected, who may be hurting, who may be grateful for some kindness and an invitation to a home or gathering.

Questions for Discussion

- Most of the participants should have brought with them to the study an object, song, poem, or story that they associate with anticipating the birth of Christ. Ask them to share this with the group and explain why it suggests to them the experience of waiting for Christ.
- Tell about a time when you met people and had the opportunity to invite them into your home or into your circle of friends. How did it feel to you to be the person who welcomed a stranger?

Robb shares these Bible verses:

He defends the cause of the fatherless and the widow, and loves the foreigner residing among you, giving them food and clothing. And you are to love those who are foreigners, for you yourselves were foreigners in Egypt.

Deuteronomy 10:18-19

- The experience of being a stranger has been a major theme in the history of the Hebrew people. God teaches them never to forget this story and to use it to prompt themselves to care about the most vulnerable. What stories in the Bible, or from church history, nudge us to notice the hidden people and to care about those who need it most?
- Can you tell us about a time when someone made a small gesture (such as the young mother who greeted her older neighbor every morning), and it made a great difference to you?
- What are some small gestures you might make toward someone that could make them feel more noticed and more a part of things (in the neighborhood, in church, other places)?
- In the book's first chapter, Robb reminds us that building and maintaining relationships is how we live and grow in faith. When showing care to people who are in need or vulnerable, are you or your church able to establish a relationship with them? What makes that easy? Or difficult?

41

- Have you participated in helping the poor or neglected during Advent, such as serving a meal to a community in need? How does that affect how you feel about the season of Advent?

Closing Prayer

Ask people to share, briefly, one or two prayer requests for celebration or for help or healing. Remind the group not to raise names of people known to others in the congregation who have not given permission or have not shared their prayer request publicly. Further, all prayer requests, like all discussion in these sessions, should be confidential.

Lead the group in prayer with either the one below or another.

> *God, you have been a traveler and you have been a refuge. You have led your people into strange lands, where they did not know where they were headed or how long the journey would take. You have provided them your security when they have felt afraid. Help us not forget that Mary, Joseph, and Jesus had those experiences. Use this to remind us to extend your welcome to the strangers in our world.*
>
> *We pray for the concerns and joys we shared today. [Speak aloud the prayer concerns or raise them in a more general way.]*
>
> *These we ask as people who wait and trust that Christ comes to renew hope in our lives. In the name of Jesus we pray. Amen.*

Prepare them for the next session:

- Thank the group for their contributions to the discussion.

- Remind them to read chapter 3 for the next session.
- Ask them to bring something that gives light, be it a candle, a flashlight, or something else.

Offer a blessing to them, such as, "May God welcome you, care for you, and fill you with the strength to do the same for others."

Encourage participants to exchange signs and words of peace with one another as they leave.

Be sure to extinguish the candle. If meeting online, remind participants to extinguish their candles.

Session 3

LEAVE THE
LIGHT ON

Opening the Session

- Welcome participants.
- Remind participants briefly about the meeting room environment (see the introduction to this study), especially if the meeting is a virtual (online) one.
- Remind them briefly about their covenant.

Theme Verse

"Arise, shine, for your light has come,
and the glory of the LORD rises upon you.
See, darkness covers the earth
and thick darkness is over the peoples,
but the LORD rises upon you
and his glory appears over you."

Isaiah 60:1-2

Session Goals

The conversations and activities in this session will equip participants to

- describe the ways in which light is an image of hope and healing.
- notice those who are invisible to others.
- determine ways in which they can "leave the light on" for others who feel lost in darkness.

Reading Assignments

Before this session, participants should read

- chapter 3 from *Making Room*
- John 1:1-13

Encourage them to read these when they have time to read them carefully and pray over them. Remind them a few days in advance of the session to read the passages, if they have not yet had time to do so. They should also bring something that gives light, such as a candle, flashlight, or something else.

Centering Prayer

Light the candle and invite participants to center their spirits and hearts for this time of worship as you pray.

> *You, O God, brought light into the world at creation and through a star that points us to Jesus Christ. Send us again that light that scares away all darkness and evil, that we may be instruments of your hope and mercy to others. In the name of Jesus, our light and life, we pray. Amen.*

Scripture

Read aloud the following Scripture passages: Isaiah 60:1-3; John 1:1-13; Psalm 36:5-9.

Give participants a minute or two to ponder these passages. Then pray:

You show us the path of life through your Holy Spirit. May our eyes and hearts follow that light as we make ourselves aware of your presence and what you have to show us today. Amen.

Biblical Insights

Invite participants to discuss these or other questions. Be sure to keep track of time so that the group has the opportunity to discuss the reading as well. Ask fewer questions if the group is particularly inclined to share their thoughts and experiences.

- What word, phrase, or idea from these readings stood out for you? What thoughts or feelings did it raise for you?
- What are some different ways you hear *light* used in these verses? Read these passages again as a reminder of what they said.

Reread aloud (or invite a participant to do so) John 1:1-4.

- This is a very poetic statement. It comes at the beginning of the Gospel of John and appears instead of a more narrative story of Jesus's coming to earth. What would you say it means?
- How would you explain it to someone?

[handwritten: When you're down and out, you don't see other's hurts, b/c you're hurting.]

[handwritten: message version]

[handwritten: verse 10, you & hospitable]

- One might say that Psalm 36:5-9 paints a picture of hospitality. Do you see any evidence of hospitality in these verses? *[handwritten: — God leaves a light on. — God is hospitable]*

The people of Israel had lost their way during their time in exile and had forgotten how the law requires compassion and concern for those who are pushed to the bottom rung of the social ladder. The prophet let them know that God noticed and that turning away from their selfish and careless ways would give them another chance to live as God's people.

[handwritten: Eph. 5:13-14]

- Reread Isaiah 60:1, what do you suppose the prophet is telling the people?
- Who is the bringer of light in this verse? *[handwritten: — How about verse 3]*
- What has "brought light" to you and helped you return to God after you have drifted away?

Review of the Session's Readings

Robb tells us that the tagline for Motel 6, "we'll leave the light on for you," always makes him think that this is what Christ followers are to do: let our lights shine in an otherwise dark world. Leaving a light on for travelers at night helps them know when they've arrived. It offers a warm glow that welcomes them in for food and rest. Perhaps when you have headed home on a dark night, you have been comforted to see a light in the window.

That the darkness can seem overwhelming became evident to Robb when he was a child. He and his family visited Carlsbad Caverns in New Mexico. At one point during the tour, when he and others were deep below ground, the park ranger turned off all the lights in the cave. The darkness was complete—leaving

Robb eager for the lights to come back on again—until the ranger lit a single match. This one match lit up the entire cave.

God's love does the same, Robb says. When darkness was everywhere, God spoke light into being. And the Bible tells us that the light was good. It was as if God had struck a single match, and it lit up the world, overcoming all darkness.

People experience darkness in their lives from time to time. They speak of having dark nights of the soul, of wandering in the dark, of being in a dark place. This suggests uncertainty, aloneness, abandonment, despair.

We are aware of darkness that rolls into the world. Wars, cold-blooded mass killings, abuse, torture, bullying, lying, racism, and more can make us wonder if the world, particularly the human race, can be redeemed. Apparently, God believes we can, for God sent us Jesus. Jesus himself said, "I am the light of the world. Whoever follows me will never walk in darkness, but will have the light of life" (John 8:12). The light of God can scatter the darkness in our hearts.

It is the poor, the chronically ill, people with disabilities, anyone who seems "different" who tend to get pushed away from light and warmth. Robb points out that Jesus came for everyone, and especially the lonely, the strangers, the isolated, the outcast, the ostracized. The people who feel most hidden in the darkness are the ones for whom Jesus "leaves the light on." Jesus erases human-drawn circles, Robb says, and creates circles that are big enough for everyone, especially those whom nobody else wants.

Jesus, after all, was born to a poor family. The first people to whom the angels announced his birth were mere shepherds, the invisible nobodies of society. His family went on the run when the powerful Herod sought to kill their infant son. As an adult, with his twelve closest disciples, he relied on the hospitality of the townspeople or other simple ways for food and shelter. He did not live an extravagant life.

So when he reached out to the poor, people with disabilities, the sinners, and those who were just not privileged enough to attend to the ritual laws, he knew what it was like to be treated as unimportant—even scorned. At Jesus's table, these folks were honored guests.

Bringing to our minds a popular practice of passing candlelight from one worshiper to the next during Christmas Eve services, Robb urges us to pass the light to one another in order to cut through the darkness. Sometimes we walk in a figurative darkness, not knowing where we can find comfort, rest, and belonging. God has left a light on for us, Robb says. Jesus draws us to him, ready to receive us with joy.

Questions for Discussion

- What does the idea of "light" mean to you? Have there been times in your life when light was very important?
- Was there ever a time when you experienced being in total darkness, such as Robb experienced in Carlsbad Caverns? What did that feel like?
- Tell about a time when you felt as though your heart and life were in a dark place. What, if anything, dispelled that darkness for you?
- Have you ever gotten lost while traveling? How did you find your way back?
- What are some ways in which you have "passed your light" to another person who may have been experiencing a time of personal darkness?

- What does it feel like to pass God's light to others, to share the love of God that you have experienced?
- What are some ways in which you have sought to bring God's light of love to other parts of the world, in those places fraught with violence, fear, and oppression?

Closing Prayer

Invite participants to briefly share reasons for celebration as well as their concerns. Remind the group not to raise names of people known to others in the congregation who have not given permission or have not shared their prayer request publicly. Further, all prayer requests, like all discussion in these sessions, should be confidential.

Ask them to join in silent prayer in their hearts as you lead them.

> *Creator God, who, with a word, brought light into the world, send the Holy Spirit as a light to us today.*
>
> *We praise you and humbly offer you gratitude for these celebrations that shine in our lives:*
> *[Observe several seconds of silence.]*
>
> *We pray for those who grieve.*
> *[Observe several seconds of silence.]*
>
> *We pray for those who suffer.*
> *[Observe several seconds of silence.]*
>
> *We pray for those who search for love and a place to call home.*
> *[Observe several seconds of silence.]*

*We pray for our leaders and that you would give them
the light of wisdom.
[Observe several seconds of silence.]*

*For the light you send to the world, that overcomes all
darkness, we praise you. We thank you that we can carry
that light to others. Let us pass your light to others so that
it will bring food to the hungry, health to the sick, love to
the fearful, and safety for the oppressed. In the name of
Jesus, whose life is light for all people. Amen.*

Prepare them for the next session:

- Thank the group for their contributions to the discussion.
- Remind them to read chapter 4 for the next session.
- Encourage them to rely on one another if they find themselves in a dark place during this season.
- Ask if someone plays guitar (or piano, if a piano is available). Ask that person if they are willing to accompany the group in singing Advent songs at the next session.

Offer a sending forth, such as: "Go in peace to love and serve the Lord."

Invite participants to exchange signs and words of peace with one another as they leave.

Be sure to extinguish the candle. If meeting online, remind participants to extinguish their candles.

Session 4

WALK EACH OTHER HOME

Opening the Session

- Welcome participants.
- Remind participants briefly about the meeting room environment (see the introduction to this study), especially if the meeting is a virtual (online) one.
- Remind them briefly about their covenant.

Theme Verse

When he was at the table with them, he took bread, gave thanks, broke it and began to give it to them. Then their eyes were opened and they recognized him, and he disappeared from their sight. They asked each other, "Were not our hearts burning within us while he talked with us on the road and opened the Scriptures to us?"

Luke 24:30-32

Session Goals

The conversations and activities in this session will equip participants to

- name the ways in which Jesus has accompanied them through life.
- describe how, through Jesus's birth, God draws us back into loving relationship with God and the community of faith.
- claim and act upon their calling to guide others to God.

Reading Assignments

Before this session, participants should read

- chapter 4 from *Making Room*
- Luke 24:13-32

Encourage them to read these when they have time to read them carefully and pray over them. Remind them a few days in advance of the session to read the passages, if they have not yet had time to do so.

Centering Prayer

Light the candle and invite participants to center their spirits and hearts for this time of worship as you pray.

> *Our God and our Guide, you walk beside us as we ponder together your truths and your mysteries. Point us to your words of life that they would be for us the compass that keeps us on your path. In the name of Christ, our Morning Star, we pray. Amen.*

Scripture

Read aloud the following Scripture passages: Luke 15:11-32; Exodus 16:1-18; Psalm 119:1-8, 105.

Give participants a minute or two to ponder these passages. Then pray:

> *God of the known and unknown, we—like the people of Israel, who wandered the desert for forty years; like Jesus, who was tested in the desert for forty days—sometimes wonder where we are headed. We make plans for our lives, but life is not controlled by our wishes. What we think we understand about life and the world is an illusion compared to your knowledge. Yet you have created us with your image in our souls. As we move forward through the deserts and the oases, not knowing where we will find them, we take courage and comfort in knowing that you walk alongside us, and your people are our spiritual companions as well. You never abandon us. Give us wisdom and courage to be that companion for others as well. Amen.*

Biblical Insights

Invite participants to discuss these or other questions. Be sure to keep track of time so that the group has the opportunity to discuss the reading as well. Ask fewer questions if the group is particularly inclined to share their thoughts and experiences.

The Luke passage tells the story of the prodigal son, which some of you may know. A son leaves home and squanders the money from his inheritance, leaving himself in absolute poverty. When he returns home, preparing to ask his father to hire him as a field hand, his father sees him "while he was still a long way off" and runs to him with joy. His brother, however, has been very loyal and reliable and resents the attention paid his brother.

- Do you identify with a character in the story? Which one, and why?
- When talking with his obedient son about the wayward son, the obedient son refers to his brother as "this son of yours." The father refers to him as "this brother of yours." Why do you suppose Jesus tells the story that way?
- Have you ever had a falling-out with a friend or family member and then reconciled? What led you to reconcile? How did that feel?
- The Exodus passage tells a central story in Judaism, one that they celebrate at the annual Passover feast. The Israelites are absolutely dependent on God. What do you think it might feel like to be part of a group that wanders for forty years in an unknown place?
- Where do you think God was when the people were hungry and tired and adrift?
- Psalm 119:105 says, "Your word is a lamp for my feet, / a light on my path." We might say that God's Word is like a flashlight in a dark forest, pointing the way ahead, one step at a time. How do you think this applies to your life?
- A lamp is sometimes used as an image of wisdom. How do you see that metaphor's significance in the verse?
- How do you observe God's wisdom shaping your spiritual life?

Review of the Session's Readings

Recalling stories of people who have traveled far from home, Robb describes a common experience in the spiritual life. Sometimes we take a wrong turn in life and are desperate to go back to where we were. Or we made the correct turn, but it still must take us through unknown territory where we know no one, do not understand the way they do things, and are not sure of how to get to a place that feels safe and familiar. Perhaps we want to serve God and those who are outcasts in this world, but no one around us wants to help or believes it is important.

Robb starts with the story of *Robinson Crusoe*, Daniel Defoe's novel about an adventurer who gets shipwrecked on a remote island and lives there for twenty-eight years. He has parrots and other animals for companions, but they do not replace human reaction. It's an achingly lonely life.

Can you imagine how desperate Robinson Crusoe must have been for rescue? Do you sometimes seek to be released from a frightening or lonely situation? God knows what this is like. It is for such as us, and the poor and outcast, that God sent Jesus to guide us out of spiritual darkness and into hope. It is not Jesus's birth alone that fulfills this rescue mission. He performs this throughout his life. The Pharisees, who made it a priority to follow the letter of the law as much as they possibly could, criticized Jesus for associating with sinners and outcasts rather than avoiding contact with them. Jesus said to them, "It is not the healthy who need a doctor, but the sick. I have not come to call the righteous, but sinners" (Mark 2:17).

We just reflected on the story of the prodigal son. It reminds us that we have forgotten who we are and whose we are when we lose our way or pursue a path that looks good at first but turns out to be a dead end of waste and superficial relationships. When we turn back—the biblical meaning of *repent*—God is already coming down the path to walk us back home.

No one avoids this. Everyone needs to be rescued. We have all wandered down that sparkling path that leads to despair or disillusionment. We give in to selfishness and greed and exploit rather than respect others. When we "come to ourselves," we realize how much we've damaged ourselves and others by taking this route.

If we open our eyes and watch, we may see that God sends a guide to help us get back on track, to walk us home.

A beautiful example of spiritual companionship is the story of the walk to Emmaus, related in Luke 24. After Jesus was resurrected, two men walked the road to Emmaus, talking and trying to make sense of what had happened over the past three days. A stranger came along and joined them. When they told him what they were puzzling over, the stranger began reviewing Moses and the prophets. He explained what was said in all the Scriptures concerning himself. That's right—eventually they realized their companion was Jesus. Afterward they asked themselves, "Were not our hearts burning within us while he talked with us on the road and opened the Scriptures to us?" (Luke 24:32).

Jesus walks us back home, but he also came to call us into community as people of faith. We have not only God but also one another. God made us to be part of a community, not isolated individuals trying to find our way on our own.

Because we were lost and now are found, we can help others find their way back. Others have helped us; we can help others. God has helped us; we can walk others back home to God.

Questions for Discussion

- Tell about a time you got lost in the woods, an unfamiliar town, or somewhere else. What did that feel like?

- Have you been through a time in your life when you felt adrift or anxious and someone came alongside to be present with you? Share the story, if you are willing.

- [Leader: read aloud Luke 24:13-35.] The disciples didn't recognize the stranger (who spoke with them and who fed them) until he blessed the meal, then "their eyes were opened and they recognized him." Why do you suppose that act helped the two recognize their companion as Jesus?

- After Jesus left them, the two disciples asked each other, "Were not our hearts burning within us while he talked with us on the road and opened the Scriptures to us?" Have you had a time when you had a very strong sense of God's closeness? If so, did this happen while you were alone or with others? What difference has such an experience made in your life?

- When someone came to be present with you while you struggled with a concern, what was most helpful to you?

- American author F. Scott Fitzgerald wrote in his book *The Crack-Up* (1945; New York: New Directions, 2009): "In a real dark night of the soul it is always three o'clock in the morning"

(p. 75). What do you suppose he meant by this? Do you think any Bible characters had such an experience?

- Home might be the place where you live now or where you grew up. Home might also be another place, such as with a group of friends, at church, a place you like to visit, or other. What makes that place "home" for you? What are the conditions that make you feel "at home"?
- How might you help someone else feel at home spiritually?
- How might you provide a sense of comfort and welcome to someone who finds Advent and Christmas to be a difficult season?
- How might you provide some moments of rest for those who find the season excessively busy?
- How will you take time for yourself to practice the lessons of Advent, either this year or in future years?
- Thinking back on what the group discussed, do you see yourself "walking someone home"? In what ways?

Hymn Singing

To celebrate the work and sharing this group has done over the past four weeks, consider leading a hymn sing. You can find Advent hymns in *The United Methodist Hymnal*, starting at hymn 196. If someone in the group plays guitar (or piano, if one is available), ask them to accompany the group.

Some hymns participants might know:

- "Come, Thou Long-Expected Jesus" (196)
- "People Look East" (202)
- "Hail to the Lord's Anointed" (203)
- "I Want to Walk as a Child of the Light" (206)
- "O Come, O Come Emmanuel" (211)
- "Lo, How a Rose E'er Blooming" (216)

Invite them to suggest others.

Closing Prayer

Invite participants to briefly share reasons for celebration as well as their concerns. Invite them to mention aloud specific requests at the prayer's cues. Remind the group not to raise names of people known to others in the congregation who have not given permission or have not shared their prayer request publicly. Further, all prayer requests, like all discussion in these sessions, should be confidential.

> *God, you walk with us in the cold dark nights and the sunny warm days of life. We are grateful for these blessings in our lives, both large and small.*
> *[Cue participants]*
>
> *We thank you for friends and family.*
> *[Cue participants]*
>
> *We thank you for those who helped us when we felt discouraged or lost.*
> *[Cue participants]*
>
> *We pray for those who feel down during Advent and Christmas.*
> *[Cue participants]*
>
> *We pray for those who are far from home.*
> *[Cue participants]*

We pray for those who are sick or suffering.
[Cue participants]

We thank you for the signs of hope you send us.
[Cue participants]

We thank you for the opportunities we have to be a friend to others.
[Cue participants]

You gave us so much in your son, Jesus. We look ahead to that season with open hearts and open eyes for those who cross our paths who might need a friend. You are a friend to us, and you walk us home. We praise you for your eternal love for all of creation. In the name of the Christ who is coming, we pray. Amen.

Close the study by thanking the group for their contributions to the discussions.

Offer a sending forth, such as: "Be the friend and companion that Christ is for you."

Encourage participants to exchange signs and words of peace with one another as they leave.

Be sure to extinguish the candle. If meeting online, remind participants to extinguish their candles.